Popular Baby Boy Names In the United States

By: Jennifer Flexser

Popular Baby Boy Names in the United States

ISBN: 978-1-60332-050-4

Edited By: Brooke Winger

Printed in the United States of America

Table of Contents

Top Ten Boy Names
in the U.S.
of the Last Century

Listed 1st to 10th

Top 10 Names From 1900 to 1909

John – William – James – George – Charles – Robert
Joseph – Frank – Edward – Thomas

1900	1901
John	John
William	William
James	James
George	George
Charles	Charles
Robert	Joseph
Joseph	Robert
Frank	Frank
Edward	Edward
Henry	Henry

1902	1903
John	John
William	William
James	James
George	George
Charles	Charles
Robert	Joseph
Joseph	Robert
Frank	Frank
Edward	Edward
Henry	Thomas

1904	1905
John	John
William	William
James	James
George	George
Robert	Charles
Charles	Robert
Joseph	Joseph
Frank	Frank
Edward	Edward
Henry	Thomas

1906	1907
John	John
William	William
James	James
George	George
Robert	Robert
Charles	Charles
Joseph	Joseph
Frank	Frank
Edward	Edward
Thomas	Henry

1908	1909
John	John
William	William
James	James
George	George
Robert	Robert
Joseph	Joseph
Charles	Charles
Frank	Frank
Edward	Edward
Thomas	Thomas

Top 10 Names in the 1910's

John – William – James – Robert – Joseph – George
Charles – Edward – Frank – Thomas

1910	1911
John	John
James	William
William	James
Robert	George
George	Robert
Joseph	Joseph
Charles	Charles
Frank	Frank
Edward	Edward
Henry	Thomas

1912	1913
John	John
William	William
James	James
Robert	Robert
Joseph	Joseph
George	George
Charles	Charles
Edward	Edward
Frank	Frank
Thomas	Thomas

1914	**1915**
John	John
William	William
James	James
Robert	Robert
Joseph	Joseph
George	George
Charles	Charles
Edward	Edward
Frank	Frank
Walter	Thomas

1916	**1917**
John	John
William	William
James	James
Robert	Robert
Joseph	Joseph
Charles	George
George	Charles
Edward	Edward
Frank	Frank
Thomas	Thomas

1918	**1919**
John	John
William	William
James	James
Robert	Robert
Charles	Charles
George	George
Joseph	Joseph
Edward	Edward
Frank	Frank
Thomas	Thomas

Top Names in the 1920's

Robert – John – James – William – Charles – George
Joseph – Richard – Edward – Donald

1920	1921
John	John
William	Robert
Robert	William
James	James
Charles	Charles
George	George
Joseph	Joseph
Edward	Edward
Frank	Frank
Richard	Richard

1922	1923
John	John
Robert	Robert
William	William
James	James
Charles	Charles
George	George
Joseph	Joseph
Edward	Edward
Richard	Richard
Frank	Donald

1924	1925
Robert	Robert
John	John
William	William
James	James
Charles	Charles
George	George
Joseph	Joseph
Richard	Richard
Edward	Edward
Donald	Donald

1926	1927
Robert	Robert
John	John
James	James
William	William
Charles	Charles
George	Richard
Richard	George
Joseph	Donald
Donald	Joseph
Edward	Edward

1928	1929
Robert	Robert
John	James
James	John
William	William
Charles	Charles
Richard	Richard
Donald	Donald
George	George
Joseph	Joseph
Edward	Edward

Top Names in the 1930's

Robert – James – John – William – Richard – Charles
Donald – George – Thomas – Joseph

1930	1931
Robert	Robert
James	James
John	John
William	William
Richard	Richard
Charles	Charles
Donald	Donald
George	George
Joseph	Joseph
Edward	Thomas

1932	1933
Robert	Robert
James	James
John	John
William	William
Richard	Richard
Charles	Charles
Donald	Donald
George	George
Joseph	Joseph
Thomas	Thomas

1934	1935
Robert	Robert
James	James
John	John
William	William
Richard	Richard
Donald	Charles
Charles	Donald
George	George
Thomas	Thomas
Joseph	Joseph

1936	**1937**
Robert	Robert
James	James
John	John
William	William
Richard	Richard
Charles	Charles
Donald	Donald
Thomas	David
George	Thomas
David	George

1938	**1939**
Robert	Robert
James	James
John	John
William	William
Richard	Richard
Charles	Charles
Donald	David
David	Donald
Thomas	Thomas
Ronald	Ronald

Top Names of the 1940's

James – Robert – John – William – Richard – David
Charles – Thomas – Michael – Ronald

1940	1941
James	James
Robert	Robert
John	John
William	William
Richard	Richard
Charles	Charles
David	David
Thomas	Thomas
Donald	Ronald
Ronald	Donald

1942	1943
James	James
Robert	Robert
John	John
William	William
Richard	Richard
David	David
Charles	Charles
Thomas	Thomas
Ronald	Ronald
Donald	Michael

1944	1945
James	James
Robert	Robert
John	John
William	William
Richard	Richard
David	David
Charles	Charles
Thomas	Thomas
Michael	Michael
Ronald	Ronald

1946	1947
James	James
Robert	Robert
John	John
William	William
Richard	Richard
David	David
Michael	Michael
Thomas	Thomas
Charles	Charles
Ronald	Larry

1948	1949
James	James
Robert	Robert
John	John
William	William
David	Michael
Michael	David
Richard	Richard
Thomas	Thomas

Charles	Charles
Ronald	Larry

Top Names of the 1950's

James – Michael – Robert – John – David – William
Richard – Thomas – Mark – Charles

1950	1951
James	James
Robert	Robert
John	John
Michael	Michael
David	David
William	William
Richard	Richard
Thomas	Thomas
Charles	Charles
Gary	Gary

1952	**1953**
James	Robert
Robert	James
John	Michael
Michael	John
David	David
William	William
Richard	Richard
Thomas	Thomas
Charles	Charles
Gary	Gary

1954	**1955**
Michael	Michael
James	David
Robert	James
John	Robert
David	John
William	William
Richard	Richard
Thomas	Thomas
Gary	Mark
Charles	Steven

1956	**1957**
Michael	Michael
James	James
Robert	David
David	Robert
John	John
William	William
Richard	Mark
Mark	Richard
Thomas	Thomas
Steven	Steven

1958	**1959**
Michael	Michael
David	David
James	James
Robert	John
John	Robert
William	Mark
Mark	William
Richard	Richard
Thomas	Thomas
Steven	Steven

Top Ten Names of the 1960's

Michael – David – John – James – Robert – Mark
William – Richard – Thomas – Jeffery

1960	1961
David	Michael
Michael	David
James	John
John	James
Robert	Robert
Mark	Mark
William	William
Richard	Richard
Thomas	Thomas
Steven	Steven

1962	1963
Michael	Michael
David	John
John	David
James	James
Robert	Robert
Mark	Mark
William	William
Richard	Richard
Thomas	Thomas
Jeffery	Jeffrey

1964	**1965**
Michael	Michael
John	John
David	David
James	James
Robert	Robert
Mark	William
William	Mark
Richard	Richard
Thomas	Thomas
Jeffery	Jeffery

1966	1967
Michael	Michael
David	David
James	James
John	John
Robert	Robert
William	William
Mark	Mark
Richard	Richard
Jeffery	Christopher
Thomas	Brian

1968	1969
Michael	Michael
David	David
John	James
James	John
Robert	Robert
William	William
Mark	Christopher
Richard	Mark
Christopher	Brian
Brian	Richard

Top Ten Names of the 1970's

Michael – Christopher – Jason – David – James – John
Robert – Brian – William – Matthew

1970	1971
Michael	Michael
James	James
David	David
John	John
Robert	Robert
Christopher	Christopher
William	William
Brian	Jason
Mark	Brian
Richard	Scott

1972	1973
Michael	Michael
Christopher	Christopher
James	Jason
David	James
John	David
Robert	John
Jason	Robert
Brian	Brian
William	William
Matthew	Matthew

1974	**1975**
Michael	Michael
Jason	Jason
Christopher	Christopher
David	James
James	David
John	Robert
Robert	John
Brian	Brian
Matthew	Matthew
William	William

1976	**1977**
Michael	Michael
Jason	Jason
Christopher	Christopher
David	David
James	James
John	Robert
Robert	John
Brian	Brian
Matthew	Matthew
Daniel	Joseph

1978	1979
Michael	Michael
Jason	Christopher
Christopher	Jason
David	David
James	James
Matthew	Matthew
John	John
Robert	Robert
Brian	Joshua
Joseph	Brian

Top Ten Names of the 1980's

Michael – Christopher – Matthew – Joshua – David – James
Daniel – Robert – John – Joseph

1980	1981
Michael	Michael
Christopher	Christopher
Jason	Matthew
David	Jason
James	David
Matthew	Joshua
Joshua	James
John	John
Robert	Robert
Joseph	Daniel

1982	1983
Michael	Michael
Christopher	Christopher
Matthew	Matthew
Jason	David
David	Joshua
James	James
Joshua	Jason
John	Daniel
Robert	John
Daniel	Robert

1984	1985
Michael	Michael
Christopher	Christopher
Matthew	Matthew
Joshua	Joshua
David	Daniel
Daniel	David
James	James
John	Robert
Robert	John
Joseph	Joseph

1986	**1987**
Michael	Michael
Christopher	Christopher
Matthew	Matthew
Joshua	Joshua
David	David
Daniel	Andrew
James	Daniel
Andrew	James
Robert	Justin
John	Robert

1988	**1989**
Michael	Michael
Christopher	Christopher
Matthew	Matthew
Joshua	Joshua
Andrew	David
David	Daniel
Justin	Andrew
Daniel	Justin
James	James
Robert	Robert

Top Ten Names of the 1990's

Michael – Christopher – Matthew – Joshua – Jacob – Nicholas
Andrew – Daniel – Tyler – Joseph

1990	1991
Michael	Michael
Christopher	Christopher
Matthew	Matthew
Joshua	Joshua
Daniel	Andrew
David	Daniel
Andrew	James
James	David
Justin	Joseph
Joseph	John

1992	1993
Michael	Michael
Christopher	Christopher
Matthew	Matthew
Joshua	Joshua
Andrew	Tyler
Brandon	Brandon
Daniel	Daniel
Tyler	Nicholas
James	Jacob
David	Andrew

1994	1995
Michael	Michael
Christopher	Matthew
Matthew	Christopher
Joshua	Jacob
Tyler	Joshua
Brandon	Nicholas
Jacob	Tyler
Daniel	Brandon
Nicholas	Daniel
Andrew	Austin

1996	1997
Michael	Michael
Matthew	Jacob
Jacob	Matthew
Christopher	Christopher
Joshua	Joshua
Nicholas	Nicholas
Tyler	Brandon
Brandon	Andrew
Austin	Austin
Andrew	Tyler

1998	**1999**
Michael	Jacob
Jacob	Michael
Matthew	Matthew
Joshua	Joshua
Christopher	Christopher
Nicholas	Nicholas
Brandon	Andrew
Tyler	Joseph
Austin	Tyler
Andrew	Daniel

Top Ten Names in the 2000's

Jacob – Michael – Joshua – Matthew – Andrew – Christopher
Daniel – Joseph – Ethan – Nicholas

2000	2001
Jacob	Jacob
Michael	Michael
Matthew	Matthew
Joshua	Joshua
Christopher	Christopher
Nicholas	Nicholas
Andrew	Andrew
Joseph	Joseph
Daniel	Daniel
Tyler	William

2002	2003
Jacob	Jacob
Michael	Michael
Joshua	Joshua
Matthew	Matthew
Ethan	Andrew
Andrew	Ethan
Joseph	Joseph
Christopher	Daniel
Nicholas	Christopher
Daniel	Anthony

2004	**2005**
Jacob	Jacob
Michael	Michael
Joshua	Joshua
Matthew	Matthew
Ethan	Ethan
Andrew	Andrew
Daniel	Daniel
William	Anthony
Joseph	Christopher
Christopher	Joseph

2006	
Jacob	
Michael	
Joshua	
Ethan	
Matthew	
Daniel	
Christopher	
Andrew	
Anthony	
William	

Top 5 Names in the Last Decade (2006-1997): Divided by State

Alaska

2006	1.James (65) 2.Jacob (53) 3. Michael (52) 4. Andrew (51) 5. Ethan (51)
2005	1.Ethan (63) 2.Jacob (58) 3.Joshua (55) 4.Michael (51) 5.William (49)
2004	1.Ethan (65) 2.Joseph (62) 3.James (59) 4.Jacob (54) 5.Samuel (54)
2003	1.Jacob (60) 2.Joseph (60) 3.Joshua (58) 4.James (55) 5.Ethan (52)
2002	1.Jacob (75) 2.Joshua (68) 3.Michael (68) 4.Ethan (56) 5.Tyler (55)
2001	1.Michael (67) 2.Jacob (66) 3.Tyler (62) 4.Ethan (61) 5.Joseph (57)
2000	1.Michael (74) 2.Jacob (68) 3.William (65)

	4.Joshua (58) 5.James (57)
1999	1.Jacob (96) 2.Joshua (77) 3.Michael (73) 4.Tyler (59) 5.Dylan (58)
1998	1.Michael (78) 2.Jacob (74) 3.Joshua (68) 4.Brandon (64) 5.David (62)
1997	1.Jacob (86) 2.James (83) 3.Michael (81) 4.Joshua (75) 5.Joseph (59)

Alabama

2006	1.William (604) 2.Jacob (431) 3.James (419) 4.Joshua (370) 5.John (369)
2005	1.William (550) 2.James (396) 3.Joshua (393) 4.John (385) 5.Michael (380)
2004	1.William (638) 2.Jacob (461) 3.John (421) 4.Joshua (398) 5.James (387)
2003	1.William (616)

	2.Jacob (461) 3.Joshua (440) 4.James (407) 5.John (388)
2002	1.William (618) 2.Jacob (456) 3.Joshua (412) 4.James (405) 5.John (378)
2001	1.William (616) 2.Jacob (493) 3.Joshua (448) 4.James (427) 5.Christopher (418)
2000	1.William (654) 2.Jacob (612) 3.Joshua (502) 4.Christopher (455) 5.Michael (450)
1999	1.William (671) 2.Jacob (532) 3.Christopher (506) 4.Austin (504) 5.John (468)
1998	1.William (701) 2.Jacob (596) 3.Austin (594) 4.Christopher (524) 5.Joshua (521)
1997	1.William (594) 2.Christopher (560) 3.James (540) 4.Jacob (530) 5.Joshua (525)

Arkansas

2006	1.William (257) 2.Ethan (242) 3.Jacob (237) 4.Landon (197) 5.James (196)
2005	1.Ethan (256) 2.William (230) 3.Jacob (226) 4.James (189) 5.Michael (188)
2004	1.Jacob (257) 2.William (249) 3.Ethan (240) 4.Joshua (236) 5.Michael (227)
2003	1.Jacob (286) 2.Ethan (265) 3.Joshua (264) 4.William (227) 5.Michael (218)
2002	1.Jacob (327) 2.Ethan (250) 3.William (240) 4.Caleb (219) 5.Joshua (211)
2001	1.Jacob (327) 2.William (250) 3.Joshua (247) 4.Austin (220) 5.Ethan (218)
2000	1.Jacob (378) 2.William (265) 3.Michael (249) 4.Joshua (240)

	5.Christopher (227)
1999	1.Jacob (339) 2.William (272) 3.Matthew (266) 4.Austin (263) 5.Michael (248)
1998	1.Jacob (372) 2.Austin (288) 3.Michael (275) 4.Joshua (274) 5.Christopher (271)
1997	1.Jacob (374) 2.Austin (314) 3.Christopher (294) 4.Michael (286) 5.Tyler (282)

Arizona

2006	1.Angel (629) 2.Daniel (592) 3.Jacob (590) 4.Anthony (588) 5.Jose (567)
2005	1.Angel (613) 2.Jacob (591) 3.Jose (581) 4.Daniel (528) 5.Michael (521)
2004	1.Jose (623) 2.Jacob (596) 3.Anthony (577) 4.Daniel (573) 5.Angel (538)

2003	1.Jacob (672) 2.Jose (629) 3.Daniel (563) 4.Anthony (554) 5.Michael (547)
2002	1.Jacob (639) 2.Jose (636) 3.Michael (605) 4.Daniel (535) 5.Joshua (525)
2001	1.Jacob (653) 2.Michael (596) 3.Jose (560) 4.Anthony (504) 5.Matthew (494)
2000	1. Jacob (680) 2.Michael (619) 3.Daniel (570) 4.Jose (541) 5.Anthony (494)
1999	1.Jacob (744) 2.Michael (619) 3.Jose (597) 4.Daniel (542) 5.Christopher (500)
1998	1.Jacob (789) 2.Michael (647) 3.Jose (614) 4.Daniel (561) 5.Anthony (484)
1997	1.Jacob (696) 2.Michael (628) 3.Daniel (576) 4.Jose (544) 5.Christopher (503)

California

2006	1.Daniel (3,754) 2..Anthony (3,720) 3.Angel (3,639) 4.Jacob (3,147) 5.David (3,087)
2005	1.Daniel (3,883) 2.Anthony (3,719) 3.Angel (3,494) 4.David (3,245) 5.Joshua (3,190)
2004	1.Daniel (4,149) 2.Anthony (3,789) 3.Andrew (3,467) 4.Jose (3,374) 5.Jacob (3,321)
2003	1.Daniel (4,019) 2.Anthony (3,921) 3.Andrew (3,441) 4.Jose (3,373) 5.Jacob (3,353)
2002	1.Daniel (4,119) 2.Anthony (3,764) 3.Jose (3,549) 4.Andrew (3,545) 5.Jacob (3,372)
2001	1.Daniel (4,151) 2.Anthony (3,818) 3.Andrew (3,442) 4.Jose (3,420) 5.Jacob (3,374)
2000	1.Daniel (4,335) 2.Anthony (3,830) 3.Jose (3,799)

	4.Andrew (3,595) 5.Michael (3,560)
1999	1.Daniel (4,347) 2.Jose (3,862) 3.Anthony (3,805) 4.Michael (3,752) 5.Andrew (3,596)
1998	1.Daniel (4,313) 2.Jose (4,274) 3.Michael (4,125) 4.Anthony (3,880) 5.Jacob (3,562)
1997	1.Daniel (4,444) 2.Michael (4,305) 3.Jose (4,152) 4.Anthony (3,909) 5.Christopher (3,765)

Colorado

2006	1.Jacob (386) 2.Ethan (319) 3.Alexander (313) 4.Joshua (308) 5.Noah (304)
2005	1.Jacob (386) 2.Joshua (369) 3.Alexander (346) 4.Joseph (338) 5.Ethan (326)
2004	1.Jacob (422) 2.Joshua (380) 3.Ethan (360) 4.Daniel (349) 5.Alexander (335)

2003	1.Jacob (477) 2.Joshua (404) 3.Andrew (385) 4.Alexander (348) 5.Daniel (348)
2002	1.Jacob (492) 2.Joshua (405) 3.Michael (396) 4.Ethan (387) 5.Joseph (348)
2001	1.Jacob (527) 2.Michael (596) 3.Jose (560) 4.Anthony (504) 5.Matthew (494)
2000	1.Jacob (517) 2.Michael (442) 3.Joshua (424) 4.Matthew (372) 5.Ryan (367)
1999	1.Jacob (568) 2.Michael (619) 3.Jose (597) 4.Daniel (542) 5.Christopher (500)
1998	1.Jacob (530) 2.Michael (497) 3.Joshua (401) 4.Matthew (397) 5.Tyler (388)
1997	1.Jacob (604) 2.Michael (492) 3.Matthew (436) 4.Austin (407) 5.Joshua (400)

Connecticut

2006	1.Michael (296) 2.Matthew (292) 3.Ryan (288) 4.Nicholas (281) 5.Anthony (269)
2005	1.Ryan (354) 2.Matthew (345) 3.Michael (344) 4.Nicholas (302) 5.Anthony (262)
2004	1.Michael (407) 2.Ryan (405) 3.Matthew (386) 4.Nicholas (318) 5.Joseph (304)
2003	1.Matthew (443) 2.Michael (441) 3.Ryan (374) 4.Nicholas (369) 5.Joseph (307)
2002	1.Michael (476) 2.Matthew (416) 3.Nicholas (397) 4.Ryan (342) 5.Christopher (338)
2001	1.Michael (489) 2.Matthew (457) 3.Nicholas (388) 4.Christopher (359) 5.John (342)
2000	1.Michael (553) 2.Matthew (461)

	3.Nicholas (439) 4.Christopher (387) 5.Ryan (369)
1999	1.Matthew (589) 2.Michael (556) 3.Nicholas (438) 4.Christopher (415) 5.John (410)
1998	1.Michael (636) 2.Matthew (532) 3.Nicholas (422) 4.Christopher (396) 5.Ryan (381)
1997	1.Michael (616) 2.Matthew (585) 3.Nicholas (457) 4.Christopher (422) 5.Daniel (374)

District of Columbia

2006	1.William (109) 2.Michael (89) 3.Christopher (76) 4.Alexander (70) 5.Anthony (69)
2005	1.William (111) 2.John (97) 3.James (80) 4.Michael (79) 5.Alexander (78)
2004	1.William (109) 2.John (96) 3.Alexander (84) 4.Joshua (78)

	5.Anthony (77)
2003	1.Michael (100) 2.William (93) 3.Alexander (80) 4.John (80) 5.David (73)
2002	1.Michael (113) 2.William (105) 3.James (82) 4.John (78) 5.David (76)
2001	1.Michael (108) 2.John (100) 3.William (96) 4.Christopher (79) 5.Joshua (79)
2000	1.John (113) 2.Christopher (107) 3.William (105) 4.Michael (102) 5.Anthony (88)
1999	1.Michael (119) 2.William (107) 3.Christopher (92) 4.John (89) 5.David (82)
1998	1.Michael (129) 2.Christopher (94) 3.John (93) 4.William (93) 5.Matthew (87)
1997	1.Michael (131) 2.John (102) 3.William (91) 4.David (89) 5.James (87)

Delaware

2006	1.Ryan (74) 2.Michael (71) 3.Jacob (67) 4.John (67) 5.Matthew (67)
2005	1.Michael (89) 2.Matthew (77) 3.Ryan (75) 4.Joshua (74) 5.Anthony (72)
2004	1.Ryan (101) 2.Michael (97) 3.Joshua (83) 4.Matthew (81) 5.Nicholas (80)
2003	1.Michael (98) 2.Andrew (87) 3.Matthew (87) 4.Ryan (84) 5.John (81)
2002	1.Matthew (100) 2.Nicholas (87) 3.Michael (84) 4.Jacob (78) 5.John (78)
2001	1.Michael (107) 2.Jacob (95) 3.Matthew (88) 4.Zachary (78) 5.Ryan (76)
2000	1.Michael (139) 2.Matthew (105)

	3.Jacob (99) 4.Joshua (95) 5.Nicholas (94)
1999	1.Michael (114) 2.Joshua (108) 3.Ryan (103) 4.Matthew (101) 5.Andrew (97)
1998	1.Michael (121) 2.Tyler (101) 3.Matthew (100) 4.Joshua (95) 5.Christopher (92)
1997	1.Michael (148) 2.Matthew (114) 3.Tyler (100) 4.Joshua (90) 5.Christopher (86)

Florida

2006	1.Joshua (1,459) 2.Michael (1,430) 3.Anthony (1,374) 4.Christopher (1,318) 5.Jacob (1,242)
2005	1.Joshua (1494) 2.Michael 1,489) 3.Anthony (1,321) 4.Christopher (1,305) 5.Jacob (1,257)
2004	1.Michael (1,583) 2.Joshua (1,498) 3.Jacob (1,321) 4.Anthony (1,286)

	5.Daniel (1,253)
2003	1.Michael (1,682) 2.Joshua (1,522) 3.Matthew (1,327) 4.Anthony (1,292) 5.Jacob (1,276)
2002	1.Michael (1,608) 2.Joshua (1,468) 3.Jacob (1,326) 4.Matthew (1,305) 5.Daniel (1,285)
2001	1.Michael (1,668) 2.Jacob (1,445) 3.Christopher (1,402) 4.Joshua (1,374) 5.Matthew (1,335)
2000	1.Michael (1,828) 2.Joshua (1,589) 3.Christopher (1,465) 4.Matthew (1,349) 5.Jacob (1,337)
1999	1.Michael (1,898) 2.Joshua (1,512) 3.Christopher (1,499) 4.Matthew (1,467) 5.Jacob (1,440)
1998	1.Michael (2,049) 2.Christopher (1,643) 3.Joshua (1,544) 4.Matthew (1,453) 5.Jacob (1,428)
1997	1.Michael (2,089) 2.Christopher (1,661) 3.Joshua (1,519) 4.Matthew (1,477) 5.Brandon (1,408)

Georgia

2006	1.William (1,004) 2.Joshua (901) 3.Christopher (787) 4.Jacob (743) 5.Michael (711)
2005	1.William (1,028) 2.Joshua (903) 3.Christopher (794) 4.Jacob (781) 5.Michael (753)
2004	1.William (1,173) 2.Joshua (890) 3.Jacob (835) 4.Christopher (807) 5.Michael (770)
2003	1.William (1,166) 2.Joshua (935) 3.Jacob (922) 4.Michael (827) 5.Christopher (809)
2002	1.William (1,112) 2.Joshua (961) 3.Jacob (924) 4.Christopher (844) 5.Michael (816)
2001	1.William (1,119) 2.Jacob (948) 3.Joshua (928) 4.Michael (922) 5.Christopher (914)
2000	1.William (1,105) 2.Christopher (1,004)

	3.Jacob (988) 4.Michael (924) 5.Joshua (902)
1999	1.William (1,178) 2.Jacob (1,036) 3.Joshua (1,035) 4.Michael (988) 5.Christopher (969)
1998	1.William (1,146) 2.Christopher (1,000) 3.Michael (997) 4.Joshua (986) 5.Jacob (979)
1997	1.Christopher (1,088) 2.Michael (1,023) 3.William (1,002) 4.Joshua (978) 5.Jacob (969)

Hawaii

2006	1.Noah (94) 2.Joshua (88) 3.Ethan (75) 4.Dylan (72) 5.Elijah (66)
2005	1.Joshua (93) 2.Jacob (89) 3.Noah (85) 4.Ethan (71) 5.Elijah (67)
2004	1.Joshua (113) 2.Noah (98) 3.Ethan (86) 4.Jacob (82)

	5.Elijah (78)
2003	1.Joshua (104) 2.Jacob (97) 3.Noah (96) 4.Ethan (83) 5.Dylan (82)
2002	1.Joshua (123) 2.Ethan (93) 3.Noah (88) 4.Isaiah (79) 5.Jacob (78)
2001	1.Joshua (108) 2.Jacob (90) 3.Matthew (79) 4.Noah (79) 5.Dylan (71)
2000	1.Joshua (131) 2.Noah (115) 3.Jacob (101) 4.Justin (92) 5.Matthew (86)
1999	1.Joshua (126) 2.Noah (108) 3.Justin (92) 4.Dylan (85) 5.Tyler (85)
1998	1.Joshua (135) 2.Matthew (103) 3.Noah (100) 4.Christopher (86) 5.Austin (83)
1997	1.Joshua (161) 2.Michael (115) 3.Tyler (115) 4.Justin (105) 5.Jacob (94)

Iowa

2006	1.Ethan (251) 2.Jacob (236) 3.Noah (212) 4.Logan (205) 5.Andrew (204)
2005	1.Ethan (286) 2.Jacob (279) 3.Logan (217) 4.Andrew (214) 5.Tyler (185)
2004	1.Jacob (292) 2.Ethan (261) 3.Logan (224) 4.Andrew (210) 5.Samuel (202)
2003	1.Jacob (331) 2.Ethan (295) 3.Tyler (236) 4.Andrew (214) 5.Logan (214)
2002	1.Jacob (376) 2.Ethan (288) 3.Tyler (237) 4.Zachary (223) 5.Austin (222)
2001	1.Jacob (433) 2.Tyler (263) 3.Logan (245) 4.Ethan (228) 5.Nicholas (226)
2000	1.Jacob (481) 2.Tyler (282)

	3.Austin (273) 4.Zachary (257) 5.Nicholas (251)
1999	1.Jacob (480) 2.Austin (332) 3.Tyler (297) 4.Nicholas (288) 5.Zachary (266)
1998	1.Jacob (507) 2.Austin (384) 3.Tyler (328) 4.Matthew (276) 5.Nicholas (270)
1997	1.Jacob (513) 2.Austin (447) 3.Tyler (347) 4.Zachary (320) 5.Nicholas (314)

Idaho

2006	1.Ethan (118) 2.Jacob (108) 3.Joshua (105) 4.Noah (104) 5.Logan (99)
2005	1.Ethan (134) 2.Jacob (131) 3.Gabriel (96) 4.Michael (91) 5.Samuel (91)
2004	1.Ethan (162) 2.Tyler (117) 3.Jacob (113) 4.Logan (102)

	5.Samuel (100)
2003	1.Ethan (159) 2.Jacob (149) 3.Tyler (108) 4.Andrew (97) 5.Logan (96)
2002	1.Jacob (148) 2.Ethan (145) 3.Tyler (112) 4.Austin (107) 5.Andrew (101)
2001	1.Jacob (180) 2.Ethan (116) 3.Joshua (109) 4.Andrew (107) 5.Michael (101)
2000	1.Jacob (162) 2.Joshua (114) 3.Joseph (110) 4.Michael (110) 5.Ethan (105)
1999	1.Jacob (182) 2.Tyler (131) 3.Austin (124) 4.Michael (110) 5.Matthew (104)
1998	1.Jacob (188) 2.Michael (142) 3.Austin (139) 4.Tyler (127) 5.Joshua (120)
1997	1.Jacob (198) 2.Austin (183) 3.Tyler (138) 4.Joshua (123) 5.Matthew (122)

Illinois

2006	1.Daniel (981) 2.Michael (954) 3.Jacob (929) 4.Alexander (913) 5.Joshua (879)
2005	1.Jacob (1,109) 2.Michael (1,101) 3.Daniel (1,068) 4.Alexander (988) 5.Matthew (972)
2004	1.Michael (1,262) 2.Jacob (1,243) 3.Daniel (1,143) 4.Anthony (1,042) 5.Joshua (1,012)
2003	1.Michael (1,333) 2.Jacob (1,246) 3.Daniel (1,098) 4.Joseph (1,075) 5.Anthony (1,070)
2002	1.Michael (1,426) 2.Jacob (1,370) 3.Matthew (1,156) 4.Daniel (1,132) 5.Joshua (1,049)
2001	1.Michael (1,446) 2.Jacob (1,421) 3.Matthew (1,337) 4.Daniel (1,181) 5.Nicholas (1,132)
2000	1.Jacob (1,593)

	2.Michael (1,540) 3.Matthew (1,389) 4.Daniel (1,260) 5.Nicholas (1,190)
1999	1.Michael (1,763) 2.Jacob (1,637) 3.Matthew (1,472) 4.Daniel (1,310) 5.Nicholas (1,299)
1998	1.Michael (1,932) 2.Jacob (1,648) 3.Matthew (1,525) 4.Nicholas (1,388) 5.Daniel (1,274)
1997	1.Michael (2,009) 2.Jacob (1,573) 3.Nicholas (1,514) 4.Matthew (1,494) 5.Daniel (1,329)

Indiana

2006	1.Jacob (568) 2.Ethan (534) 3.Andrew (436) 4.Michael (425) 5.William (415)
2005	1.Jacob (668) 2.Ethan (640) 3.Andrew (463) 4.Joshua (455) 5.Michael (426)
2004	1.Jacob (684) 2.Ethan (632) 3.Andrew (486)

	4.Michael (470) 5.Joshua (469)
2003	1.Jacob (771) 2.Ethan (659) 3.Michael (518) 4.Andrew (511) 5.Joshua (491)
2002	1.Jacob (774) 2.Ethan (658) 3.Michael (508) 4.Joshua (505) 5.Austin (493)
2001	1.Jacob (938) 2.Ethan (587) 3.Andrew (563) 4.Michael (562) 5.Joshua (544)
2000	1.Jacob (1,054) 2.Austin (639) 3.Andrew (636) 4.Michael (608) 5.Zachary (589)
1999	1.Jacob (1,131) 2.Austin (760) 3.Tyler (642) 4.Nicholas (625) 5.Michael (619)
1998	1.Jacob (1,120) 2.Austin (804) 3.Michael (739) 4.Tyler (127) 5.Joshua (120)
1997	1.Jacob (1,128) 2.Austin (912) 3.Michael (736) 4.Tyler (695)

	5.Zachary (669)

Kansas

2006	1.Jacob (221) 2.Ethan (212) 3.Logan (198) 4.Alexander (191) 5.William (177)
2005	1.Jacob (264) 2.Ethan (251) 3.Andrew (188) 4.Joseph (174) 5.Logan (173)
2004	1.Jacob (290) 2.Ethan (245) 3.Michael (203) 4.Alexander (193) 5.Andrew (189)
2003	1.Jacob (275) 2.Ethan (273) 3.Andrew (219) 4.Joshua (199) 5.Tyler (189)
2002	1.Jacob (317) 2.Ethan (288) 3.Andrew (234) 4.Joshua (216) 5.Zachary (215)
2001	1.Jacob (343) 2.Michael (224) 3.Ethan (222) 4.Andrew (212) 5.Austin (208)

2000	1.Jacob (405) 2.Michael (250) 3.Tyler (239) 4.Joshua (238) 5.Zachary (238)
1999	1.Jacob (451) 2.Austin (267) 3.Joshua (243) 4.Michael (242) 5.Matthew (229)
1998	1.Jacob (432) 2.Austin (279) 3.Matthew (260) 4.Zachary (251) 5.Michael (242)
1997	1.Jacob (407) 2.Austin (324) 3.Michael (273) 4.Matthew (250) 5.Nicholas (249)

Kentucky

2006	1.Jacob (491) 2.William (453) 3.Ethan (421) 4.James (364) 5.Landon (338)
2005	1.Jacob (550) 2.Ethan (462) 3.William (402) 4.James (396) 5.Joshua (347)
2004	1.Jacob (478)

	2.Ethan (391) 3.William (370) 4.James (336) 5.Logan (278)
2003	1.Jacob (618) 2.James (453) 3.Ethan (434) 4.William (428) 5.Joshua (368)
2002	1.Jacob (624) 2.Ethan (498) 3.William (485) 4.James (418) 5.Austin (385)
2001	1.Jacob (711) 2.William (502) 3.Austin (418) 4.James (399) 5.Ethan (383)
2000	1.Jacob (804) 2.William (508) 3.Austin (500) 4.James (475) 5.Michael (468)
1999	1.Jacob (732) 2.Austin (605) 3.William (549) 4.James (460) 5.Matthew (447)
1998	1.Jacob (845) 2.Austin (742) 3.William (523) 4.James (502) 5.Matthew (474)
1997	1.Austin (729) 2.Jacob (720)

	3.James (538) 4.William (516) 5.Matthew (483)

Louisiana

2006	1.Landon (308) 2.Ethan (307) 3.Joshua (278) 4.Jacob (268) 5.Christopher (267)
2005	1.Ethan (321) 2.Joshua (318) 3.Michael (309) 4.Jacob (304) 5.William (269)
2004	1.Ethan (375) 2.Joshua (369) 3.Jacob (355) 4.Michael (330) 5.Christopher (310)
2003	1.Jacob (421) 2.Ethan (384) 3.Joshua (378) 4.Michael (338) 5.Christopher (333)
2002	1.Jacob (409) 2.Joshua (409) 3.Michael (398) 4.Ethan (352) 5.Christopher (330)
2001	1.Jacob (426) 2.Joshua (407) 3.Michael (389)

	4.Christopher (365) 5.Matthew (345)
2000	1.Joshua (471) 2.Jacob (438) 3.Christopher (430) 4.Michael (426) 5.Tyler (399)
1999	1.Joshua (460) 2.Jacob (451) 3.Christopher (429) 4.Michael (405) 5.Tyler (399)
1998	1.Jacob (494) 2.Joshua (481) 3.Michael (465) 4.Austin (461) 5.Christopher (444)
1997	1.Joshua (538) 2.Michael (500) 3.Christopher (485) 4.Tyler (454) 5.Jacob (443)

Massachusetts

2006	1.Matthew (585) 2.Ryan (566) 3.Michael (556) 4.Nicholas (505) 5.Andrew (485)
2005	1.Matthew (693) 2.Michael (642) 3.Ryan (631) 4.Nicholas (543) 5.John (518)

2004	1.Michael (751) 2.Matthew (721) 3.Ryan (720) 4.Nicholas (610) 5.Andrew (547)
2003	1.Matthew (779) 2.Michael (777) 3.Ryan (711) 4.Nicholas (692) 5.John (615)
2002	1.Matthew (889) 2.Michael (874) 3.Nicholas (398) 4.Ethan (352) 5.Christopher (330)
2001	1.Matthew (915) 2.Michael (904) 3.Nicholas (792) 4.Ryan (746) 5.John (731)
2000	1.Matthew (1,038) 2.Michael (1,015) 3.John (814) 4.Nicholas (797) 5.Ryan (705)
1999	1.Matthew (1,007) 2.Michael (991) 3.Nicholas (868) 4.John (802) 5.Ryan (768)
1998	1.Michael (1,174) 2.Matthew (1,135) 3.Nicholas (1,009) 4.John (746) 5.Ryan (718)

| 1997 | 1.Matthew (1,169)
2.Michael (1,119)
3.Nicholas (1,006)
4.Christopher (803)
5.John (797) |

Maryland

2006	1.Joshua (458) 2.Michael (449) 3.William (405) 4.Jacob (400) 5.Matthew (378)
2005	1.Joshua (460) 2.Michael (459) 3.Ryan (415) 4.William (415) 5.Matthew (412)
2004	1.Michael (507) 2.Jacob (472) 3.Joshua (464) 4.Ryan (430) 5.Matthew (424)
2003	1.Joshua (535) 2.Michael (516) 3.Jacob (490) 4.Ryan (484) 5.Andrew (434)
2002	1.Michael (552) 2.Jacob (517) 3.Matthew (517) 4.Joshua (500) 5.Christopher (459)
2001	1.Michael (600) 2.Matthew (534)

	3.Joshua (520) 4.Jacob (502) 5.Nicholas (457)
2000	1.Michael (618) 2.Joshua (553) 3.Jacob (541) 4.Matthew (531) 5.Ryan (525)
1999	1.Michael (686) 2.Matthew (599) 3.Jacob (565) 4.Joshua (542) 5.Ryan (505)
1998	1.Michael (711) 2.Jacob (646) 3.Matthew (607) 4.Nicholas (537) 5.Joshua (504)
1997	1.Michael (761) 2.Matthew (648) 3.Joshua (546) 4.Christopher (533) 5.Nicholas (532)

Maine

2006	1.Jacob (126) 2.Ethan (108) 3.Benjamin (100) 4.Tyler (87) 5.Logan (82)
2005	1.Jacob (123) 2.Tyler (97) 3.Alexander (87) 4.Benjamin (85)

	5.Andrew (84)
2004	1.Jacob (111) 2.Ethan (109) 3.Samuel (101) 4.Benjamin (95) 5.Caleb (92)
2003	1.Jacob (137) 2.Nicholas (106) 3.Joshua (104) 4.Matthew (97) 5.Ethan (93)
2002	1.Jacob (153) 2.Ethan (121) 3.Joshua (103) 4.Nicholas (102) 5.Samuel (96)
2001	1.Jacob (201) 2.Matthew (118) 3.Nicholas (117) 4.Ethan (111) 5.Cameron (109)
2000	1.Jacob (166) 2.Nicholas (130) 3.Joshua (114) 4.Tyler (111) 5.Matthew (108)
1999	1.Jacob (187) 2.Nicholas (167) 3.Tyler (136) 4.Zachary (129) 5.Matthew (114)
1998	1.Jacob (211) 2.Nicholas (147) 3.Tyler (144) 4.Matthew (124) 5.Joshua (121)

1997	1.Jacob (177) 2.Nicholas (167) 3.Tyler (160) 4.Matthew (143) 5.Joshua (142)

Michigan

2006	1.Jacob (847) 2.Ethan (723) 3.Logan (653) 4.Michael (651) 5.Andrew (650)
2005	1.Jacob (947) 2.Andrew (809) 3.Ethan (780) 4.Joshua (683) 5.Michael (669)
2004	1.Jacob (1,164) 2.Ethan (851) 3.Andrew (781) 4.Michael (780) 5.Joshua (742)
2003	1.Jacob (1,194) 2.Ethan (859) 3.Joshua (840) 4.Michael (834) 5.Andrew (816)
2002	1.Jacob (1,300) 2.Joshua (870) 3.Ethan (869) 4.Michael (856) 5.Nicholas (822)
2001	1.Jacob (1,380)

	2.Nicholas (947) 3.Joshua (933) 4.Michael (921) 5.Andrew (894)
2000	1.Jacob (1,568) 2.Joshua (1,010) 3.Michael (996) 4.Nicholas (967) 5.Andrew (935)
1999	1.Jacob (1,736) 2.Michael (1,077) 3.Nicholas (1,020) 4.Tyler (1,004) 5.Joshua (997)
1998	1.Jacob (1,761) 2.Michael (1,196) 3.Joshua (1,078) 4.Austin (1,068) 5.Nicholas (1,051)
1997	1.Jacob (1,748) 2.Michael (1,373) 3.Austin (1,224) 4.Tyler (1,177) 5.Nicholas (1,100)

Minnesota

2006	1.Ethan (462) 2.Jacob (446) 3.Logan (410) 4.Benjamin (398) 5.Jack (397)
2005	1.Ethan (492) 2.Jacob (474)

	3.Samuel (440) 4.Jack (420) 5.Andrew (414)
2004	1.Jacob (520) 2.Ethan (464) 3.Samuel (447) 4.Andrew (436) 5.Tyler (407)
2003	1.Jacob (589) 2.Ethan (496) 3.Joseph (451) 4.Andrew (449) 5.Samuel (448)
2002	1.Jacob (619) 2.Ethan (495) 3.Benjamin (459) 4.Samuel (457) 5.Nicholas (452)
2001	1.Jacob (719) 2.Samuel (509) 3.Joseph (487) 4.Benjamin (480) 5.Andrew (477)
2000	1.Jacob (748) 2.Nicholas (536) 3.Matthew (510) 4.Andrew (501) 5.Samuel (491)
1999	1.Jacob (753) 2.Nicholas (549) 3.Matthew (537) 4.Benjamin (514) 5.Andrew (501)
1998	1.Jacob (801) 2.Matthew (605) 3.Nicholas (579)

	4.Tyler (526) 5.Andrew (521)
1997	1.Jacob (822) 2.Matthew (656) 3.Nicholas (628) 4.Andrew (569) 5.Austin (523)

Missouri

2006	1.Jacob (550) 2.Logan (449) 3.Andrew (442) 4.Ethan (440) 5.William (426)
2005	1.Jacob (542) 2.Ethan (497) 3.William (459) 4.Andrew (447) 5.Tyler (424)
2004	1.Jacob (657) 2.Ethan (542) 3.Andrew (494) 4.Tyler (453) 5.Michael (439)
2003	1.Jacob (716) 2.Ethan (494) 3.Tyler (491) 4.Andrew (481) 5.William (458)
2002	1.Jacob (758) 2.Ethan (529) 3.Andrew (512) 4.Austin (462)

	5.Joshua (455)
2001	1.Jacob (828) 2.Andrew (504) 3.Michael (499) 4.Austin (496) 5.Matthew (487)
2000	1.Jacob (899) 2.Tyler (581) 3.Michael (577) 4.Matthew (546) 5.Nicholas (517)
1999	1.Jacob (984) 2.Austin (667) 3.Andrew (584) 4.Matthew (583) 5.Michael (575)
1998	1.Jacob (1,031) 2.Austin (741) 3.Tyler (654) 4.Michael (633) 5.Nicholas (582)
1997	1.Jacob (1,011) 2.Austin (799) 3.Tyler (655) 4.Michael (640) 5.Zachary (605)

Mississippi

2006	1.William (309) 2.James (298) 3.Joshua (250) 4.Christopher (237) 5.John (234)

2005	1.William (336) 2.James (286) 3.John (237) 4.Christopher (233) 5.Jacob (232)
2004	1.William (354) 2.James (284) 3.John (257) 4.Joshua (247) 5.Michael (242)
2003	1.William (334) 2.Christopher (295) 3.James (279) 4.Jacob (263) 5.Joshua (249)
2002	1.William (336) 2.Christopher (297) 3.James (286) 4.Joshua (286) 5.Jacob (248)
2001	1.William (339) 2.James (288) 3.Jacob (282) 4.Michael (277) 5.Christopher (273)
2000	1.William (391) 2.James (327) 3.Christopher (316) 4.Michael (270) 5.Jacob (269)
1999	1.William (336) 2.James (333) 3.Christopher (330) 4.Joshua (315) 5.Michael (305)
1998	1.James (383)

	2.William (380) 3.Christopher (334) 4.Austin (301) 5.Joshua (301)
1997	1.William (378) 2.Christopher (357) 3.James (341) 4.Joshua (336) 5.John (305)

Montana

2006	1.Jacob (68) 2.Logan (61) 3.Michael (60) 4.William (60) 5.James (55)
2005	1.Jacob (84) 2.Ethan (72) 3.Michael (59) 4.Joseph (55) 5.Logan (53)
2004	1.Jacob (71) 2.Ethan (64) 3.William (62) 4.Michael (57) 5.Joseph (56)
2003	1.Jacob (81) 2.Ethan (65) 3.Joshua (65) 4.Hunter (63) 5.Logan (62)
2002	1.Ethan (79) 2.Jacob (65) 3.Dylan (63)

	4.Logan (62) 5.Tyler (61)
2001	1.Jacob (71) 2.Ethan (70) 3.Tyler (69) 4.Dylan (60) 5.Hunter (60)
2000	1.Jacob (99) 2.Tyler (76) 3.Zachary (64) 4.Michael (63) 5.Dylan (62)
1999	1.Tyler (87) 2.Jacob (85) 3.Michael (80) 4.Matthew (71) 5.Ryan (66)
1998	1.Jacob (103) 2.Austin (84) 3.Michael (81) 4.Tyler (72) 5.Cody (62)
1997	1.Jacob (121) 2.Austin (95) 3.Tyler (83) 4.Matthew (72) 5.Michael (69)

North Carolina

2006	1.William (882) 2.Joshua (826) 3.Jacob (777) 4.Christopher (734) 5.Michael (664)

2005	1.William (923) 2.Joshua (833) 3.Jacob (831) 4.Christopher (705) 5.Michael (670)
2004	1.William (955) 2.Jacob (912) 3.Joshua (861) 4.Michael (654) 5.Ethan (649)
2003	1.Jacob (1,007) 2.William (982) 3.Joshua (878) 4.Michael (743) 5.Christopher (729)
2002	1.William (1,009) 2.Jacob (979) 3.Joshua (887) 4.Christopher (776) 5.Michael (766)
2001	1.Jacob (1,016) 2.William (971) 3.Joshua (919) 4.Christopher (797) 5.Michael (784)
2000	1.William (1,043) 2.Jacob (1,038) 3.Joshua (1,009) 4.Christopher (889) 5.Michael (861)
1999	1.Jacob (1,092) 2.Joshua (1,004) 3.William (990) 4.Christopher (962) 5.Michael (954)

1998	1.William (1,055) 2.Jacob (1,045) 3.Joshua (1,019) 4.Christopher (971) 5.Michael (948)
1997	1.Christopher (1,016) 2.Joshua (1,002) 3.Michael (986) 4.William (976) 5.Jacob (975)

North Dakota

2006	1.Logan (71) 2.Ethan (63) 3.Jacob (62) 4.Carter (59) 5.Noah (58)
2005	1.Ethan (80) 2.Jacob (59) 3.Carter (53) 4.Noah (53) 5.Dylan (51)
2004	1.Ethan (84) 2.Jacob (73) 3.Andrew (57) 4.Logan (55) 5.Mason (51)
2003	1.Ethan (83) 2.Jacob (74) 3.Logan (61) 4.Hunter (56) 5.Samuel (53)
2002	1.Jacob (92)

	2.Ethan (88) 3.Logan (72) 4.Joshua (53) 5.Tyler (51)
2001	1.Jacob (89) 2.Ethan (71) 3.Matthew (62) 4.Dylan (58) 5.Hunter (54)
2000	1.Jacob (114) 2.Hunter (73) 3.Ethan (71) 4.Matthew (65) 5.Austin (61)
1999	1.Jacob (105) 2.Dylan (71) 3.Hunter (71) 4.Tyler (71) 5.Zachary (70)
1998	1.Jacob (116) 2.Matthew (89) 3.Austin (88) 4.Tyler (83) 5.Zachary (71)
1997	1.Austin (123) 2.Jacob (116) 3.Zachary (93) 4.Tyler (83) 5.Michael (76)

Nebraska

2006	1.Jacob (147) 2.Alexander (144) 3.Ethan (129)

	4.Andrew (124) 5.Logan (122)
2005	1.Jacob (169) 2.Ethan (164) 3.Samuel (126) 4.Alexander (117) 5.Joshua (113)
2004	1.Jacob (219) 2.Ethan (196) 3.Samuel (147) 4.Alexander (129) 5.Joshua (127)
2003	1.Jacob (230) 2.Ethan (183) 3.Tyler (138) 4.Alexander (136) 5.Joshua (128)
2002	1.Jacob (245) 2.Ethan (170) 3.Joshua (160) 4.Zachary (143) 5.Alexander (142)
2001	1.Jacob (287) 2.Zachary (156) 3.Ethan (152) 4.Tyler (147) 5.Joshua (141)
2000	1.Jacob (270) 2.Tyler (177) 3.Joshua (162) 4.Zachary (161) 5.Andrew (158)
1999	1.Jacob (307) 2.Tyler (194) 3.Austin (180) 4.Joshua (166)

	5.Michael (155)
1998	1.Jacob (316) 2.Austin (190) 3.Tyler (190) 4.Michael (171) 5.Zachary (167)
1997	1.Jacob (329) 2.Austin (209) 3.Tyler (186) 4.Zachary (186) 5.Matthew (184)

New Hampshire

2006	1.Jacob (118) 2.Ryan (103) 3.Benjamin (95) 4.William (92) 5.Andrew (90)
2005	1.Jacob (145) 2.Ryan (126) 3.Matthew (112) 4.Benjamin (108) 5.Tyler (98)
2004	1.Jacob (132) 2.Ryan (129) 3.Matthew (123) 4.Ethan (112) 5.Andrew (106)
2003	1.Jacob (131) 2.Ryan (130) 3.Nicholas (116) 4.Matthew (114) 5.Joshua (113)

2002	1.Jacob (147) 2.Matthew (144) 3.Nicholas (112) 4.Ethan (110) 5.Joshua (108)
2001	1.Jacob (166) 2.Matthew (130) 3.Ryan (125) 4.Tyler (121) 5.Nicholas (119)
2000	1.Jacob (197) 2.Matthew (163) 3.Ryan (146) 4.Nicholas (132) 5.Michael (127)
1999	1.Jacob (193) 2.Matthew (153) 3.Nicholas (149) 4.Tyler (140) 5.Ryan (132)
1998	1.Jacob (214) 2.Matthew (184) 3.Nicholas (166) 4.Michael (149) 5.Tyler (146)
1997	1.Nicholas (174) 2.Tyler (172) 3.Jacob (165) 4.Matthew (156) 5.Michael (148)

2006	1.Michael (1,017) 2.Matthew (894) 3.Daniel (792) 4.Joseph (783)

	5.Anthony (772)
2005	1.Michael (1,082) 2.Matthew (969) 3.Ryan (918) 4.Anthony (864) 5.Joseph (851)
2004	1.Michael (1,214) 2.Matthew (1,090) 3.Nicholas (986) 4.Ryan (938) 5.Joseph (928)
2003	1.Michael (1,338) 2.Matthew (1,226) 3.Nicholas (1,029) 4.Joseph (924) 5.Anthony (884)
2002	1.Michael (1,358) 2.Matthew (1,203) 3.Nicholas (1,042) 4.Joseph (1,017) 5.Christopher (965)
2001	1.Michael (1,414) 2.Matthew (1,288) 3.Nicholas (1,079) 4.Joseph (1,063) 5.Christopher (964)
2000	1.Michael (1,437) 2.Matthew (1,253) 3.Nicholas (1,059) 4.Christopher (1,011) 5.Joseph (986)
1999	1.Michael (1,619) 2.Matthew (1,414) 3.Nicholas (1,115) 4.Christopher (1,009) 5.Joseph (977)

1998	1.Michael (1,724) 2.Matthew (1,386) 3.Nicholas (1,190) 4.Christopher (1,102) 5.Joseph (1,018)
1997	1.Michael (1,749) 2.Matthew (1,421) 3.Nicholas (1,168) 4.Christopher (1,149) 5.Joseph (1,045)

New Mexico

2006	1.Isaiah (166) 2.Joshua (161) 3.Gabriel (160) 4.Daniel (147) 5.Joseph (147)
2005	1.Joshua (196) 2.Isaiah (188) 3.Jacob (164) 4.Daniel (155) 5.Elijah (141)
2004	1.Jacob (178) 2.Joshua (173) 3.Matthew (165) 4.Daniel (154) 5.Isaiah (154)
2003	1.Joshua (195) 2.Jacob (194) 3.Gabriel (154) 4.Jose (149) 5.Michael (149)
2002	1.Joshua (186)

	2.Jacob (181) 3.Isaiah (173) 4.Matthew (169) 5.Michael (153)
2001	1.Joshua (212) 2.Jacob (208) 3.Michael (177) 4.Isaiah (170) 5.Joseph (149)
2000	1.Jacob (216) 2.Joshua (185) 3.Isaiah (184) 4.Michael (184) 5.Matthew (159)
1999	1.Jacob (233) 2.Joshua (203) 3.Michael (188) 4.Matthew (175) 5.Isaiah (168)
1998	1.Michael (237) 2.Joshua (210) 3.Jacob (199) 4.Matthew (185) 5.Joseph (169)
1997	1.Joshua (226) 2.Christopher (206) 3.Matthew (204) 4.Jacob (198) 5.Michael (188)

Nevada

2006	1.Anthony (245) 2.Daniel (218) 3.Angel (213) 4.Jacob (184)

	5.David (174)
2005	1.Anthony (223) 2.Jacob (220) 3.Daniel (209) 4.Angel (206) 5.Joshua (205)
2004	1.Anthony (251) 2.Jacob (216) 3.Daniel (210) 4.Joshua (210) 5.Michael (196)
2003	1.Anthony (236) 2.Michael (212) 3.Jacob (207) 4.Joshua (186) 5.Joseph (173)
2002	1.Anthony (237) 2.Daniel (217) 3.Michael (213) 4.Jacob (212) 5.Christopher (194)
2001	1.Anthony (256) 2.Jacob (228) 3.Christopher (191) 4.Michael (185) 5.Daniel (183)
2000	1.Jacob (216) 2.Anthony (223) 3.Joshua (201) 4.Brandon (194) 5.Daniel (190)
1999	1.Jacob (228) 2.Michael (207) 3.Anthony (197) 4.Joshua (195) 5.Tyler (183)

1998	1.Michael (251) 2.Jacob (224) 3.Anthony (211) 4.Brandon (189) 5.Matthew (178)
1997	1.Michael (250) 2.Jacob (231) 3.Christopher (190) 4.Anthony (187) 5.Daniel (178)

New York

2006	1.Michael (1,953) 2.Matthew (1,756) 3.Joseph (1,567) 4.Anthony (1,524) 5.Christopher (1,465)
2005	1.Michael (2,080) 2.Matthew (1,829) 3.Joseph (1,667) 4.Anthony (1,616) 5.Ryan (1,591)
2004	1.Michael (2,345) 2.Matthew (2,024) 3.Joseph (1,859) 4.Daniel (1,681) 5.Ryan (1,672)
2003	1.Michael (2,449) 2..Matthew (2,113) 3.Joseph (1,955) 4.Nicholas (1,809) 5.Christopher (1,786)
2002	1.Michael (2,578)

	2.Matthew (2,115) 3.Nicholas (2,055) 4.Joseph (1,998) 5.Christopher (1,818)
2001	1.Michael (2,754) 2.Matthew (2,254) 3.Nicholas (2,072) 4.Joseph (2,030) 5.Christopher (1,944)
2000	1.Michael (2,888) 2.Matthew (2,484) 3.Nicholas (2,121) 4.Christopher (2,071) 5.Joseph (2,065)
1999	1.Michael (3,095) 2.Matthew (2,739) 3.Nicholas (1,115) 4.Christopher (1,009) 5.Joseph (977)
1998	1.Michael (3,401) 2.Matthew (2,613) 3.Nicholas (2,372) 4.Christopher (2,297) 5.Joseph (2,267)
1997	1.Michael (3,457) 2.Matthew (2,668) 3.Christopher (2,467) 4.Nicholas (2,431) 5.Joseph (2.360)

Ohio

2006	1.Jacob (1,038) 2.Andrew (920) 3.Ethan (850)

	4.Michael (838) 5.Noah (782)
2005	1.Jacob (1,176) 2.Andrew (991) 3.Ethan (941) 4.Michael (909) 5.Logan (814)
2004	1.Jacob (1,300) 2.Ethan (1,091) 3.Andrew (1,017) 4.Michael (957) 5.Matthew (890)
2003	1.Jacob (1,474) 2.Andrew (1,070) 3.Michael (1,044) 4.Ethan (991) 5.Joshua (942)
2002	1.Jacob (1,581) 2.Michael (1,156) 3.Andrew (1,048) 4.Joshua (1,014) 5.Ethan (993)
2001	1.Jacob (1,754) 2.Michael (1,206) 3.Nicholas (1,115) 4.Andrew (1,094) 5.Joshua (1,054)
2000	1.Jacob (1,880) 2.Michael (1,367) 3.Nicholas (1,220) 4.Tyler (1,206) 5.Andrew (1,191)
1999	1.Jacob (2,049) 2.Michael (1,414) 3.Austin (1,344) 4.Nicholas (1,273)

	5.Tyler (1,244)
1998	1.Jacob (2,098) 2.Michael (1,556) 3.Austin (1,423) 4.Nicholas (1,308) 5.Matthew (1,280)
1997	1.Jacob (2,034) 2.Michael (1,532) 3.Austin (1,485) 4.Nicholas (1,452) 5.Tyler (1,395)

Oklahoma

2006	1.Jacob (338) 2.Ethan (257) 3.Joshua (234) 4.William (218) 5.Michael (213)
2005	1.Jacob (328) 2.Ethan (316) 3.Joshua (263) 4.Michael (258) 5.William (235)
2004	1.Jacob (374) 2.Ethan (332) 3.Joshua (261) 4.Michael (260) 5.Tyler (251)
2003	1.Jacob (395) 2.Ethan (323) 3.Joshua (297) 4.Michael (258) 5.Caleb (243)

2002	1.Jacob (434) 2.Ethan (317) 3.Joshua (304) 4.Caleb (270) 5.Tyler (264)
2001	1.Jacob (454) 2.Joshua (318) 3.Michael (317) 4.Ethan (286) 5.Caleb (256)
2000	1.Jacob (467) 2.Tyler (357) 3.Joshua (348) 4.Matthew (329) 5.Michael (323)
1999	1.Jacob (502) 2.Joshua (357) 3.Tyler (350) 4.Matthew (332) 5.Michael (328)
1998	1.Jacob (486) 2.Austin (406) 3.Joshua (373) 4.Michael (367) 5.Tyler (367)
1997	1.Jacob (520) 2.Tyler (396) 3.Austin (380) 4.Joshua (366) 5.Michael (366)

Oregon

2006	1.Jacob (281)

	2.Ethan (257) 3.Joshua (234) 4.William (218) 5.Michael (213)
2005	1.Jacob (290) 2.Ethan (269) 3.Andrew (226) 4.Alexander (216) 5.Joshua (216)
2004	1.Jacob (290) 2.Ethan (288) 3.Daniel (227) 4.Alexander (222) 5.Andrew (217)
2003	1.Jacob (330) 2.Ethan (290) 3.Andrew (246) 4.Joshua (211) 5.Daniel (210)
2002	1.Jacob (338) 2.Ethan (331) 3.Joshua (243) 4.Michael (238) 5.Andrew (235)
2001	1.Jacob (389) 2.Joshua (306) 3.Ethan (272) 4.Michael (261) 5.Tyler (250)
2000	1.Jacob (446) 2.Joshua (298) 3.Michael (291) 4.Daniel (285) 5.Tyler (285)
1999	1.Jacob (457) 2.Michael (307)

	3.Austin (298) 4.Joshua (297) 5.Tyler (296)
1998	1.Jacob (495) 2.Austin (335) 3.Joshua (295) 4.Tyler (295) 5.Michael (294)
1997	1.Jacob (469) 2.Austin (411) 3.Michael (345) 4.Andrew (315) 5.Tyler (305)

Pennsylvania

2006	1.Jacob (1,058) 2.Michael (1,019) 3.Ryan (953) 4.Joseph (840) 5.Matthew (810)
2005	1.Michael (1,107) 2.Jacob (998) 3.Matthew (994) 4.Ryan (960) 5.Nicholas (933)
2004	1.Michael (1,236) 2.Jacob (1,096) 3.Ryan (1,070) 4.Matthew (1,050) 5.Nicholas (945)
2003	1.Michael (1,282) 2.Ryan (1,171) 3.Jacob (1,149) 4.Matthew (1,075)

	5.Nicholas (1,025)
2002	1.Michael (1,347) 2.Jacob (1,253) 3.Matthew (1,170) 4.Nicholas (1,039) 5.Ryan (1,015)
2001	1.Michael (1,437) 2.Jacob (1,297) 3.Matthew (1,271) 4.Nicholas (1,161) 5.Tyler (1,053)
2000	1.Michael (1,488) 2.Jacob (1,375) 3.Matthew (1,371) 4.Nicholas (1,284) 5.Ryan (1,161)
1999	1.Michael (1,644) 2.Matthew (1,507) 3.Nicholas (1,381) 4.Jacob (1,372) 5.Ryan (1,248)
1998	1.Michael (1,803) 2.Matthew (1,573) 3.Nicholas (1,421) 4.Jacob (1,408) 5.Tyler (1,354)
1997	1.Michael (1,794) 2.Matthew (1,676) 3.Nicholas (1,518) 4.Jacob (1,384) 5.Tyler (1,362)

Rhode Island

2006	1.Ryan (101) 2.Jacob (87) 3.Nicholas (82) 4.Michael (78) 5.Benjamin (76)
2005	1.Michael (118) 2.Matthew (100) 3.Jacob (97) 4.Ethan (93) 5.Ryan (92)
2004	1.Michael (115) 2.Matthew (111) 3.Jacob (106) 4.Alexander (99) 5.Nicholas (95)
2003	1.Michael (150) 2.Matthew (143) 3.Jacob (118) 4.Nicholas (110) 5.Ryan (108)
2002	1.Nicholas (138) 2.Michael (124) 3.Matthew (123) 4.Jacob (117) 5.Ethan (103)
2001	1.Michael (140) 2.Matthew (133) 3.Jacob (122) 4.Nicholas (118) 5.Ryan (110)
2000	1.Matthew (150) 2.Michael (146) 3.Nicholas (141) 4.Jacob (119) 5.Ryan (106)
1999	1.Matthew (163)

	2.Nicholas (161) 3.Michael (160) 4.Jacob (132) 5.Zachary (129)
1998	1.Matthew (200) 2.Nicholas (154) 3.Michael (146) 4.Jacob (142) 5.Zachary (116)
1997	1.Michael (184) 2.Nicholas (178) 3.Matthew (173) 4.Christopher (138) 5.Tyler (116)

South Carolina

2006	1.William (430) 2.Christopher (350) 3.James (341) 4.Jacob (331) 5.Joshua (320)
2005	1.William (430) 2.Jacob (355) 3.James (331) 4.Joshua (327) 5.John (307)
2004	1.William (497) 2.Jacob (393) 3.James (369) 4.Joshua (348) 5.Christopher (346)
2003	1.William (470) 2.Jacob (398) 3.James (372) 4.Joshua (357)

	5.Christopher (326)
2002	1.William (533) 2.Jacob (388) 3.Joshua (385) 4.James (375) 5.Christopher (357)
2001	1.William (530) 2.Jacob (428) 3.Joshua (397) 4.Christopher (390) 5.James (377)
2000	1.William (551) 2.Christopher (442) 3.Jacob (428) 4.Joshua (399) 5.James (398)
1999	1.William (507) 2.Joshua (434) 3.Jacob (431) 4.Michael (423) 5.James (419)
1998	1.William (528) 2.Michael (457) 3.Christopher (450) 4.Joshua (438) 5.Jacob (421)
1997	1.William (521) 2.Christopher (502) 3.Joshua (459) 4.Michael (431) 5.Austin (416)

South Dakota

2006	1.Jacob (80) 2.Ethan (76) 3.Carter (55) 4.Logan (55) 5.Landon (54)
2005	1.Jacob (80) 2.Ethan (65) 3.Carter (60) 4.Tyler (58) 5.Landon (57)
2004	1.Ethan (95) 2.Jacob (79) 3.Logan (60) 4.Mason (59) 5.Dylan (58)
2003	1.Jacob (80) 2.Ethan (70) 3.Logan (64) 4.Mason (57) 5.Carter (54)
2002	1.Jacob (102) 2.Ethan (74) 3.Mason (71) 4.Logan (69) 5.Samuel (57)
2001	1.Jacob (93) 2.Dylan (79) 3.Ethan (67) 4.Hunter (65) 5.Austin (64)
2000	1.Jacob (120) 2.Dylan (77)

	3.Austin (71) 4.Ethan (69) 5.Nicholas (65)
1999	1.Jacob (109) 2.Austin (90) 3.Tyler (89) 4.Dylan (84) 5.Logan (71)
1998	1.Austin (120) 2.Jacob (114) 3.Tyler (79) 4.Matthew (74) 5.Michael (72)
1997	1.Jacob (121) 2.Austin (105) 3.Michael (81) 4.Tyler (75) 5.Matthew (73)

Tennessee

2006	1.William (693) 2.Jacob (615) 3.Joshua (538) 4.Ethan (521) 5.James (510)
2005	1.William (743) 2.Jacob (644) 3.Ethan (597) 4.James (546) 5.Joshua (512)
2004	1.William (830) 2.Jacob (720) 3.Ethan (578) 4.Joshua (559)

	5.James (523)
2003	1.William (790) 2.Jacob (759) 3.Joshua (575) 4.James (567) 5.Ethan (554)
2002	1.Jacob (816) 2.William (749) 3.Joshua (591) 4.James (589) 5.Michael (577)
2001	1.Jacob (871) 2.William (792) 3.Joshua (643) 4.James (613) 5.Austin (556)
2000	1.Jacob (947) 2.William (867) 3.James (669) 4.Joshua (665) 5.Michael (636)
1999	1.Jacob (968) 2.William (830) 3.Austin (801) 4.Joshua (674) 5.James (659)
1998	1.Jacob (964) 2.William (848) 3.Austin (813) 4.Joshua (743) 5.Michael (725)
1997	1.Jacob (884) 2.Austin (845) 3.William (841) 4.Joshua (709) 5.Michael (702)

Texas

2006	1.Jose (2,637) 2.Jacob (2,208) 3.Joshua (2,132) 4.Daniel (2,126) 5.Christopher (2,122)
2005	1.Jose (2,792) 2.Jacob (2,297) 3.Joshua (2,210) 4.Daniel (2,095) 5.Christopher (2,030)
2004	1.Jose (2,890) 2.Jacob (2,504) 3.Joshua (2,305) 4.Daniel (2,079) 5.David (2,059)
2003	1.Jose (2,912) 2.Jacob (2,518) 3.Joshua (2,233) 4.Daniel (2,109) 5.Michael (2,102)
2002	1.Jose (3,147) 2.Jacob (2,617) 3.Joshua (2,333) 4.Michael (2,172) 5.Christopher (2,145)
2001	1.Jose (2,917) 2.Jacob (2,576) 3.Michael (2,286) 4.Joshua (2,247) 5.Christopher (2,205)
2000	1.Jose (3,093) 2.Jacob (2,823)

	3.Joshua (2,452) 4.Michael (2,432) 5.Christopher (2,274)
1999	1.Jose (2,937) 2.Jacob (2,734) 3.Michael (2,655) 4.Christopher (2,399) 5.Joshua (2,302)
1998	1.Jose (2,928) 2.Jacob (2,716) 3.Michael (2,637) 4.Christopher (2,514) 5.Joshua (2,379)
1997	1.Jose (2,934) 2.Michael (2,710) 3.Christopher (2,562) 4.Jacob (2,541) 5.Joshua (2,476)

Utah

2006	1.Ethan (344) 2.Joshua (324) 3.Jacob (312) 4.Samuel (282) 5.Benjamin (246)
2005	1.Jacob (322) 2.Ethan (317) 3.Joshua (292) 4.Samuel (262) 5.Andrew (247)
2004	1.Ethan (412) 2.Jacob (351) 3.Joshua (304)

	4.Samuel (293) 5.William (249)
2003	1.Ethan (406) 2.Jacob (355) 3.Joshua (319) 4.Samuel (281) 5.Tyler (262)
2002	1.Jacob (398) 2.Ethan (378) 3.Joshua (360) 4.Samuel (256) 5.Tyler (244)
2001	1.Jacob (424) 2.Ethan (372) 3.Joshua (347) 4.Tyler (261) 5.Michael (250)
2000	1.Jacob (438) 2.Joshua (346) 3.Ethan (333) 4.Tyler (277) 5.Zachary (277)
1999	1.Jacob (453) 2.Joshua (358) 3.Tyler (292) 4.Zachary (286) 5.Michael (280)
1998	1.Jacob (461) 2.Joshua (414) 3.Tyler (350) 4.Austin (333) 5.Michael (286)
1997	1.Jacob (470) 2.Joshua (354) 3.Tyler (351) 4.Austin (340)

	5.Michael (298)

Virginia

2006	1.William (656) 2.Jacob (614) 3.Michael (579) 4.Joshua (572) 5.Christopher (555)
2005	1.William (742) 2.Jacob (728) 3.Michael (661) 4.Joshua (627) 5.Matthew (568)
2004	1.Jacob (747) 2.William (745) 3.Joshua (654) 4.Michael (637) 5.Ethan (604)
2003	1.Jacob (795) 2.William (750) 3.Michael (725) 4.Joshua (684) 5.Christopher (633)
2002	1.Jacob (764) 2.Michael (754) 3.William (743) 4.Joshua (650) 5.Ethan (623)
2001	1.Jacob (874) 2.William (796) 3.Michael (787) 4.Joshua (712) 5.Matthew (711)

2000	1.Jacob (869) 2.William (783) 3.Michael (777) 4.Matthew (738) 5.Christopher (736)
1999	1.Jacob (910) 2.Michael (807) 3.William (777) 4.Matthew (757) 5.Christopher (704)
1998	1.Jacob (461) 2.Joshua (414) 3.Tyler (350) 4.Austin (333) 5.Michael (286)
1997	1.Michael (898) 2.Matthew (844) 3.Jacob (841) 4.Christopher (815) 5.William (762)

Vermont

2006	1.Jacob (56) 2.Noah (41) 3.William (40) 4.Owen (38) 5.Aiden (37)
2005	1.Jacob (63) 2.Connor (44) 3.Samuel (42) 4.Matthew (41) 5.Ryan (39)

2004	1.Jacob (65) 2.Ryan (46) 3.William (45) 4.Ethan (43) 5.Matthew (42)
2003	1.Ethan (60) 2.Jacob (56) 3.Benjamin (48) 4.Tyler (47) 5.William (47)
2002	1.Ethan (71) 2.Jacob (60) 3.Matthew (57) 4.Hunter (51) 5.William (47)
2001	1.Jacob (77) 2.Nicholas (49) 3.Dylan (48) 4.Ethan (47) 5.Samuel (47)
2000	1.Jacob (79) 2.Matthew (60) 3.Ryan (59) 4.Michael (52) 5.Tyler (51)
1999	1.Jacob (74) 2.Nicholas (68) 3.Matthew (63) 4.Dylan (58) 5.Ryan (54)
1998	1.Jacob (88) 2.Tyler (65) 3.Matthew (54) 4.Zachary (50) 5.Nicholas (48)
1997	1.Jacob (81)

	2.Nicholas (69) 3.Ryan (67) 4.Tyler (61) 5.Matthew (60)

Washington

2006	1.Jacob (488) 2.Alexander (463) 3.Ethan (459) 4.Daniel (397) 5.Logan (396)
2005	1.Jacob (480) 2.Ethan (441) 3.Alexander (427) 4.Andrew (395) 5.Daniel (385)
2004	1.Jacob (314) 2.Ethan (491) 3.Andrew (455) 4.Alexander (414) 5.Joshua (396)
2003	1.Jacob (538) 2.Ethan (487) 3.Joshua (426) 4.Ryan (425) 5.Alexander (408)
2002	1.Ethan (562) 2.Jacob (533) 3.Michael (431) 4.Joshua (420) 5.Alexander (416)
2001	1.Jacob (644) 2.Joshua (467) 3.Ethan (464)

	4.Michael (436) 5.Andrew (435)
2000	1.Jacob (654) 2.Michael (509) 3.Joshua (505) 4.Alexander (493) 5.Tyler (482)
1999	1.Jacob (730) 2.Michael (526) 3.Michael (528) 4.Tyler (524) 5.Matthew (500)
1998	1.Jacob (761) 2.Michael (598) 3.Austin (573) 4.Joshua (516) 5.Andrew (511)
1997	1.Jacob (713) 2.Michael (649) 3.Austin (610) 4.Andrew (552) 5.Joshua (511)

Wisconsin

2006	1.Ethan (472) 2.Jacob (446) 3.Logan (393) 4.Mason (372) 5.Alexander (350)
2005	1.Ethan (488) 2.Jacob (470) 3.Tyler (385) 4.Alexander (384)

	5.Logan (365)
2004	1.Ethan (543) 2.Jacob (534) 3.Alexander (385) 4.Tyler (370) 5.Samuel (363)
2003	1.Jacob (616) 2.Ethan (481) 3.Logan (423) 4.Tyler (407) 5.Samuel (397)
2002	1.Jacob (603) 2.Ethan (519) 3.Tyler (423) 4.Nicholas (421) 5.Joshua (412)
2001	1.Jacob (747) 2.Matthew (448) 3.Samuel (447) 4.Tyler (447) 5.Nicholas (427)
2000	1.Jacob (732) 2.Nicholas (510) 3.Tyler (497) 4.Michael (462) 5.Joshua (445)
1999	1.Jacob (853) 2.Austin (562) 3.Michael (528) 4.Tyler (524) 5.Matthew (500)
1998	1.Jacob (931) 2.Michael (559) 3.Austin (549) 4.Tyler (541) 5.Nicholas (520)

1997	1.Jacob (885) 2.Austin (585) 3.Michael (573) 4.Tyler (571) 5.Matthew (565)

West Virginia

2006	1.Jacob (197) 2.Ethan (187) 3.Logan (164) 4.Landon (135) 5.Hunter (128)
2005	1.Jacob (241) 2.Ethan (170) 3.Hunter (161) 4.Logan (133) 5.Andrew (130)
2004	1.Jacob (259) 2.Ethan (186) 3.Logan (141) 4.Tyler (140) 5.Hunter (138)
2003	1.Jacob (291) 2.Ethan (187) 3.Hunter (168) 4.Matthew (168) 5.Tyler (161)
2002	1.Jacob (268) 2.Austin (190) 3.Hunter (186) 4.Ethan (176) 5.James (165)
2001	1.Jacob (325)

	2.Austin (188) 3.Hunter (170) 4.Zachary (158) 5.Tyler (156)
2000	1.Jacob (312) 2.Austin (212) 3.Tyler (190) 4.Michael (189) 5.Joshua (176)
1999	1.Jacob (311) 2.Austin (272) 3.Tyler (205) 4.Matthew (190) 5.Joshua (182)
1998	1.Jacob (299) 2.Austin (276) 3.Tyler (208) 4.Brandon (203) 5.Michael (198)
1997	1.Jacob (298) 2.Austin (261) 3.Brandon (261) 4.Tyler (260) 5.Michael (215)

Wyoming

2006	1.Ethan (44) 2.Jacob (42) 3.Logan (41) 4.Ryan (38) 5.Hunter (34)
2005	1.Jacob (41) 2.Ethan (39) 3.Tyler (35)

	4.Michael (31) 5.Joseph (30)
2004	1.Michael (34) 2.Hunter (31) 3.Jacob (31) 4.Ethan (30) 5.Joshua (29)
2003	1.Jacob (47) 2.Ethan (42) 3.Joshua (34) 4.Matthew (34) 5.Hunter (32)
2002	1.Ethan (52) 2.Jacob (49) 3.Hunter (35) 4.Joshua (35) 5.Austin (29)
2001	1.Jacob (44) 2.Joshua (41) 3.Michael (36) 4.Tyler (35) 5.Hunter (34)
2000	1.Jacob (49) 2.Ethan (36) 3.Michael (36) 4.Matthew (33) 5.Hunter (32)
1999	1.Michael (52) 2.Austin (45) 3.Joshua (43) 4.Tyler (43) 5.Jacob (40)
1998	1.Austin (55) 2.Jacob (49) 3.Matthew (47) 4.Michael (46)

	5.Tyler (44)
1997	1.Jacob (55) 2.Austin (54) 3.Tyler (44) 4.Michael (40) 5.Cody (36)

Acknowledgements:

Social Security Online. 11 May 2007. Social Security
      Administration. 4 Dec. 2007
      http://www.ssa.gov/OACT/babynames/index.html>.

www.ingramcontent.com/pod-product-compliance
Lightning Source LLC
Chambersburg PA
CBHW051055050326
40690CB00006B/731